Perfect CV

HOW TO WRITE

THE PERFECT CV

Practical Guide with Examples

M. E. Brandon

The information included in this book is offered in good faith believing to be exact at the moment of its publication and subjected to necessary modifications.

Photographs:

Businesswoman. Author: Search Engine People Blog www.flickr.com, creativecommons.org/licenses/by/2.0/deed.es

Letter. Author: Thetaxheaven on www.flickr.com under licence creativecommons.org/licenses/by/2.0/

Perfect CV

PROLOGUE

The curriculum vitae or CV constitutes the best business card of a candidate when applying for a job. It is absolutely essential if the candidate wants to participate in the recruitment process.

This book intends to be a practical guide on how to create the perfect CV that could fulfil its main purpose: **become the best presentation tool of the candidate.** With this objective in mind, this book tries to support the candidate in his/her trip towards ideal work.

Perfect CV

The following suggestions and practical examples are the results of many years of experience as a qualified teacher in the issue and responsible for different human resources departments and numerous recruitment processes.

"There is not a second opportunity for a first impression". Oscar Wilde.

INDEX

CHAPTER I: WHAT IS A CV?	1
CHAPTER II: BEFORE WRITING	3
CHAPTER III: TYPES OF CVS	6
Chronologic CV	6
Functional CV	10
Combined CV	16
CHAPTER IV: WRITING THE PERFECT CV	16
CHAPTER V: THE COVER LETTER	39
Basic Rules in a Cover Letter	40
CHAPTER VII: THE APPLICATION FORM	61
CHAPTER VIII: APPENDIX AND EXAMPLES	71

CHAPTER I: WHAT IS A CV?

The CV is a briefing on the academic and professional life of a person, including achievements, challenges and abilities obtained throughout the years.

As it is the first image that a company has of a candidate, it is extremely important that the document is well written and edited; as well as ensuring the document contains the necessary information to convert it into the best marketing tool. Most candidates write a CV as an obligation, thinking that all employees should have one at the moment of looking for a job and, therefore, they forget that the CV is a tool that could give the candidate the job of his or her life.

Elaborating a CV could help the candidate to identify his abilities and strengths while obtaining a complete and clear vision about the path that he wants to follow in their professional career. Besides, the CV could become the ideal base for a job interview.

The CV should be concise and professional and, above all, it should be focused - as much as possible- on the professional profile required by the company. After all, those candidates that provide a perfect CV and cover letter focused on the requirements of the different job descriptions are those who eventually obtain invitations to participate in job interviews.

CHAPTER II: BEFORE WRITING

There are a number of key points to consider before sitting in front of a blank page.

1. Choose the type of work to apply for. Obviously, not everyone has a clear idea about what particular career path that they want to follow from an early age. Therefore, the candidate should develop a profound analysis on his or her working preferences with the end of avoiding multiple changes in their career that could be reflected on a CV and could be seen as a lack of security.

2. Focus the search for jobs in the selected sector and on the field in which the candidate, preferably, has either (or both) academic or professional experience.

CHAPTER III: TYPES OF CVs

Chronological CV

This type of CV is the most used by candidates. Do it from past to present because, with the passage of time, the candidate usually acquires more qualifications and/or job responsibilities- the most recent achievements being the most valued by human resources departments.

The CV should contain personal details, qualifications, professional experience, hobbies and, preferably, a mention of possible references.

It also should include a brief paragraph at the beginning of the CV that clearly and powerfully specifies the abilities, achievements, knowledge and strengths of the candidate.

The chronological CV should include the following information in this order:

- Personal details.

- A statement of knowledge, objectives and achievements.

- Academic data, preferably from present to past.

- Should you have enough professional experience, it is recommendable to introduce it before the academic qualifications.

Functional CV

The functional CV is more focused on the abilities, knowledge and achievements of the candidates. It is possibly not as clear and easy to read as the chronological one, but its results are especially useful when the candidate has little professional experience or when the candidate wants to emphasise academic achievements.

This type of CV is not centred on work experience in particular, but it describes the abilities developed and the achievements and knowledge obtained throughout the academic and/or professional life.

The functional CV will include the same information as the chronological one, but will give more attention to the candidate's strengths, showing them in order of importance.

The information introduced in this type of CV should be the following:

- Personal details.

- Personal abilities. Some examples of abilities are:

Communication Capacity

Having the ability to communicate and negotiate with others. Dealing with customers and delegates from different international congresses has helped me to develop a great communication capacity.

Team Work

Team work has allowed me to obtain a number of objectives and professional achievements as the perfect development of international congresses.

Organisation

I have great organisation capability, as well as the ability to develop planning tasks in a clear and concise manner.

Problem Solving

Ability to develop profound analysis and strategies with the objective of avoiding possible conflicts before they materialise, solving complex problems in a creative manner.

Marketing

I have participated in the development of publicity campaigns, organising all types of events and elaborating communication strategies.

Other achievements could be: elaboration of documents, team management, customer skills, planning skills, social abilities, complex decision making, ability to keep calm under stressful situations, ability to work under pressure covering strict deadlines and negotiation skills, etc.

- Academic details, preferably from present to past.

- Additional knowledge.

- Hobbies and interests (related to the job position).

- References (it's important to mention them).

The functional CV is recommended when the candidate has periods of inactivity which could be less exposed with a CV of this type.

This type of CV should be used when the candidate has changed career paths on different occasions. As this type of CV focuses on abilities and strengths, the changes in career paths are less obvious.

The functional CV is very useful when the candidate wishes to change career paths as it emphasises abilities and skills that could be easily applied in other areas.

This type of CV is also a good option when the candidate does not have enough professional experience because it emphasises skills such as working under pressure, organisation skills, maturity, emotional stability and team work.

The biggest disadvantage of the functional CV is that some people could find it difficult to expand a list and write about their abilities and achievements.

Combined CV

The combined CV includes the same information as the previous ones but mixes both types, which converts into the most complete type of CV.

The information to include in a combined CV is the following:

- Personal details.

- Achievements, knowledge and skills.

- Academic details.

- Professional experience including skills, strengths and achievements.

- Additional knowledge.

- Interests and hobbies (when related to the job position).
- References.

The combined CV is used when the candidate has a combination of academic achievements and professional experience together with a number of skills and knowledge. This type of CV could be very useful when the candidate manages to impress the person in charge of the recruitment process during the first part of the document, making it possible that the person will read the CV right to the end.

The combined CV has the disadvantage that it could not be used by every candidate. For instance, when the candidate has some periods of professional inactivity, the type of CV to use is the functional one as the chronological and combined CVs could clearly expose those inactive periods, which could be difficult to explain during the course of a job interview.

CHAPTER IV: WRITING THE PERFECT CV

1. After deciding on the type of curriculum to write, you should develop the structure of the document, this can be achieved by introducing the information in a coherent manner and in agreement with the model of CV chosen.

2. Keeping in mind that the candidate does not know the preferences of the people in charge of the recruitment process, it is a good idea to use a standard editing. In this way, the curriculum vitae should be presented in **just two A4 pages over a soft background, preferably white,** avoiding the use of colourful pages and staples.

3. The use of block letters should be limited to the start of the sentences, paragraphs and names. In any other part of the text, the block letters could be understood as shouting, which would be disrespectful towards the reader.

4. The type of font to used should be New Times Roman, Verdana or Arial, although there is certain flexibility in this regard.

5. The size of the font should be between 10 and 14, preferably 12. This is not too small so that it makes reading the document difficult and not too large to give the impression of "filling" the document.

6. It is important to pay attention to the editing of the document and try to obtain regularity regarding bold and italics, numbers and symbols.

7. It is not recommended to include the words CURRICULUM VITAE or CV at the beginning of the document as it is obvious and it could be seen as unnecessarily repetitive.

8. The information should be introduced in different sections in a clear and concise manner. It is important to avoid the use of overly complex vocabulary.

   Try placing yourself in the shoes of the reader and check that the document can be easily understood.

9. When writing the CV, it is important to bear in mind the job requirements and form a list of the skills and knowledge required for the position, relating them to the candidate's achievements, skills and experience as much as practically possible.

It is a good idea to remember that the person who grants a job interview wishes to minimise collateral damages as much as possible and, therefore, he or she will not take the risk of hiring someone who does not demonstrate skills and knowledge related to the offered job position.

At the beginning of the document, it is suggested that you include an "objective statement", or a small briefing consisting of a few lines that authoritatively describe and defend the abilities and experience of the candidate with authority.

This is probably the most difficult task in a CV, and it is essential that this paragraph is focused on each job applied for and it retains the attention of the reader in a powerful way, to make him or her think that **he or she is the person to hire.**

A good statement of objectives will include a short sentence describes the profession and experience of the candidate, followed by two or three abilities or personal characteristics and, finally, include a sentence that describes interests or professional objectives.

In this sense, you should make a list that includes five or six abilities or achievements related to the position applied for and add sentences using those abilities or achievements as starting points.

An important point to bear in mind is that the companies are not interested in what the job position could give to the candidate, but **what the candidate could bring to the company.**

An example of an objective statement could be:

- Motivated and creative executive with ten years of experience managing team works. Great problem solving skills, able to work under pressure and to analyse and plan complex financial operations.

    At the moment, I am searching for a position in the bank sector that could give me a personal and professional challenge and could give me further experience and knowledge.

10. The candidate should place himself/herself in the shoes of the reader.

Those working in the Human Resources Department may receive and read dozens of CVs every single week and, therefore, the document should include the largest amount of information in the most concise and clear manner. Remember that it is necessary to avoid boring the reader, which may cause them to stop reading. On the contrary, the objective is to "engage" the reader in such a way that he or she reads through the entire document.

A good way to avoid this common error is to focus the CV as a telegram, avoiding the use of large and complex sentences.

Remember that the objective is to make the reader interested.

11. It is important to separate the duties developed with the help of symbols or numbers.

12. The verbs to use should be action verbs that show initiative such as elaborate, develop, organise, manage and coordinate teams.

13. It is necessary to avoid the use of slang and informal vocabulary or colloquialism.

14. The sentences should be powerful, emphasising the achievements and capabilities of the candidate.

15. Avoid including information related to political or religious preferences, as it could have a negative result.

16. Do not include unemployment periods, preferences regarding salary, labour conditions, complete address of previous employers and reason for leaving the previous jobs. This information should be reserved for a possible job interview or included in an application form, if required.

17. It is important to avoid routines. For instance, when describing the tasks fulfilled in an administrative job position, it is important to avoid describing routine tasks such as making photocopies or changing the toner of the printer. Instead, it is a good idea to include action tasks like developing a database of clients and suppliers or being responsible for constant communication with suppliers and buyers.

18. The candidate should include courses, internship or volunteer work when he or she does not have enough professional experience. Further supporting documents can be provided at the interview stage. In case of participating in a lot of courses and/or conferences and congresses, it is necessary to remember that the CV is a brief document and, therefore, only the most important courses and conferences related to the job position should be included.

19. Once the candidate has enough professional experience, the information should be filtered, leaving in the most relevant and taking away any experience that is unimportant or not closely related to the selected job offer.

20. Additionally, it is important to include hobbies and interests, when positive, and if they are related to the job position. For example, if the job position requires social or artistic skills, these should be included in the CV.

When developing this section, the candidate should avoid typical sentences like "going out with friends", as well as creating a list of passive hobbies like reading, computing or painting that, although could show a certain degree of culture, are tasks that could be developed individually and could give a feeling of lack of social skills and difficulty in working as part of a close team.

On the contrary, hobbies that stand out from the norm like photo-diving could attract attention, even if they are individual activities, as they reveal an interest to the reader. Also, the practice of a sport in a semi-professional or regular manner could be positive as the sport endows people with a number of qualities such as discipline, team spirit and a constant search for perfection and improvement, which could easily be transferred to professional life.

21. **The candidate has to learn to sell himself or herself.** The aim of the CV is to obtain a job interview and, therefore, the candidate has to develop his/her own marketing campaign to ensure they are successful.

Therefore, it is convenient to never forget that this document is the first contact with a possible manager and that it is essential to attract his or her attention in just two pages and convince him or her to grant a job interview.

The curriculum should boost the skills, virtues, strengths, achievements and experience of the candidate.

22. **Be careful with lies!** Very often, candidates confuse marketing with lies, crossing the fine line that separates both concepts. Be careful and avoid this mistake that is commonly made by candidates.

If the curriculum obtains its objective and the candidate is granted a job interview, herein lies the danger, as a lie could easily be detectable, especially if the person in charge of the interview has experience in the issue.

For instance, it is not a good idea to lie about qualifications which could be required at some point during the recruitment process or about the level of a certain foreign language or a computing programme, as the person responsible for the interview could wish to practically check the knowledge of the specified language or computing skills.

23. It is important to transmit a positive attitude, trying to be honest while emphasising knowledge and achievements.

24. It is also important to mention professional references. Therefore, the candidate should contact two or three people in advance, preferably former managers or supervisors, who can offer professional references.

When the candidate does not have professional experience, usually the references are offered by tutors or teachers. Once the candidate has some professional experience to use, the academic references (except in those clearly academic CVs focused on this sector) should be replaced by professional ones.

25. When sending the curriculum vitae to a foreign country, the candidate should familiarise him or herself with the requirements of each country.

26. A common mistake is to send the curriculum to many email addresses all at the same time. Opening an email and finding a number of addresses that have received the same message will not give any credibility to the fact that the candidate is interested in one specific job position in particular, thus significantly reducing the possibility of being granted a job interview.

27. Once the document is complete, the candidate should revise the grammar and spelling. Therefore, it is convenient to print the document and read it carefully in search of errors.

A CV with spelling mistakes could give the reader the impression that the candidate is unable to write two pages, which are so important for his or her future without making mistakes, meaning he or she will not be able to create any document required as part of his or her job position.

In fact, if the CV is focused on a managerial position (or the job requires the making of documents), **a grammar mistake could be unforgettable.**

28. The final revision of the document must include the complete address of the company, as well as the complete address of the candidate, allowing the company to readily contact the candidate.

29. At the moment of checking the document, it is crucial to answer, with total honesty, a number of questions:

- Is this CV focused on the job applied for?

- Is all of the necessary information included?

- Are my achievements, virtues, knowledge, skills, experience and strengths sufficiently emphasised Is there any information that should be eliminated?

- Are my experiences, achievements and knowledge properly related to the job offered?

- What exactly is the company looking for?

Above all, it is important to put yourself in the shoes of the other person and answer: **Why should I meet with you and offer you a job interview?**

30. Finally, it is necessary to remember that most candidates make different mistakes in their CVs, one of which is not tailoring the document to the offered job. **A well written and personalised curriculum stands out among the rest,** it also naturally increase the possibility of the candidate being invited to participate in the recruitment process.

CHAPTER V: THE COVER LETTER

The cover letter is an indispensable document to be sent together with the CV if the candidate wants to have a chance of participating in the next step of any recruitment process.

Several statistics developed by official institutions and employment agencies have revealed that including a well written and presented cover letter in the application will significantly increase the chances of obtaining a job interview.

Together with the curriculum vitae, the cover letter is the business card of a candidate. Therefore, it is important that it fulfils its main objective: **be the perfect marketing tool for the candidate.**

Additionally, the cover letter is the ideal tool to show synthesis, editing and grammar skills, abilities highly valued at the moment of choosing a candidate and those which could not be widely expanded upon in the curriculum.

Before writing the letter, you should develop a small draft of the content, including all relevant information.

Basic Rules in a Cover Letter

There are a number of rules to follow at the time of writing a cover letter:

- The document should not be longer than one A4 page in a standard colour (preferably white) and with black font.

- The page should not be folded or include any piercing on the edge, being the same type of paper and colour as the one used in the attached CV.

- Never staple the cover letter to the CV.

- Usually, the type of font to use should be New Times Roman, Verdana or Arial, although there is certain flexibility on this regard. The size of the font should be between 10 and 14, preferably 12.

- The cover letter should be clear, concise and direct, written in a formal tone and being careful not to make spelling and grammar mistakes.

- The use of block letters is limited to the beginning of the sentences/paragraphs and to names, being misunderstood as a lack of respect and a sign of shouting elsewhere in the document.

- Never send a cover letter that has been written by hand (unless required by the employer) as the person in charge of the recruitment process could think that the candidate does not have knowledge of computers which, in modern times, is an indispensable requirement for any job position.

- It is fundamental that the address of the company is clearly specified and well written.

If the candidate does not know the address of the company, it is recommended to do a little research through telephone books or the Internet.

- Including the name of the person in charge of the recruitment process (sometimes it is included in the application form) significantly increases the chances of obtaining a positive answer.

It is important to contact the company and specifically ask for the name of the person in charge of the recruitment process, giving the impression of being truly interested in the offered position.

- If the letter is to be sent to an employment agency, the candidate should include the address of the agency. The applicant should bear in mind that the services of the agency have been hired to act as a filter and, therefore, the agency is responsible for the candidate offering a job interview.

- The candidate should never send photocopies of the cover letters and curriculums as the companies like to feel "special" to the applicants.

When the cover letter is sent by email, it should be included in the body of the message.

If the letter is sent as an attached document, it is essential to write a few lines in the body of the message and the document be attached with the name of "Covering Letter". In this way, the cover letter takes the risk of being identified as spam.

- It is vital that the person in charge of the recruitment process has the feeling that the applicant is clearly **interested in that position and company in particular** and not simply obtaining any job, even though this may be the case.

Transmitting interest for a particular position gives the interviewer the feeling that the applicant will be loyal to the company and, possibly, wish to develop a professional career within the company. Therefore, the time, effort and money invested in the adaptation process will be widely rewarded.

- The cover letter must be a clear and concise briefing of everything included in the curriculum. It is important not to repeat the same sentences used in the CV while capturing its essence and emphasising the most important points made in it.

- Use action verbs like organise, elaborate, coordinate, develop or manage.

- The sentences and paragraphs should be clear and short, increasing the chances that the reader continues until the end of the document.

- It is necessary to use a positive and optimistic language, emphasising achievements and skills, but being careful not to trespass the limit of arrogance or give an image of "know-it-all".

- The description of the job should be read carefully and focus given to the abilities and achievements to be described in the covering letter.

A common error consists of sending letters of presentation and curriculums which are not focused on the requirements desired by the company, giving a feeling that you are not interested and that you did not dedicate enough time and effort to produce an adequate cover letter. In this way, the applicant should ask himself or herself whether or not he or she has shown enough interest in the advertised job position.

- The candidate should transmit a sense of honesty and, therefore, it is necessary to find the appropriate balance between formal vocabulary and informal vocabulary without falling into the temptation of repeating the typical sentences that are used by most people.

Furthermore, it is necessary to avoid informal vocabulary and speaking to the reader as to a friend.

- Never include personal information like hobbies and interests, information that should be briefly included in the CV but not in the presentation letter.

- It is important to include a short paragraph that is clearly related to the company offering the job. It should also show that the candidate knows about the history and activity developed by the company in question and has a great interest in the job position.

- Once the letter is complete, the applicant should check for possible spelling and grammar errors.

If possible, the candidate should ask another person to read the document as someone who is not involved in the process is able to detect mistakes much easier.

The basic structure and content of a cover letter could be constructed as follows:

Greeting

In the first paragraph, or greeting paragraph, the applicant should introduce him or herself and explain how he or she has learnt about the offer (where and, if possible, when the advertising was read).

Some examples of "opening sentences" in a presentation letter are:

- I write regarding the job position published in the newspaper or website...

- I take the chance to contact you regarding your job offer...

- I have just finished my BA ... and I have decided to contact you regarding the job position...

- I have learnt about the activity developed by your company and I have decided to send you my CV in case you could consider it for further job positions... (this paragraph is ideal in the case of spontaneous applications).

- As you can see from my CV, which I attached...

- My name is... and I write regarding the job position published in...

Introduction

This is the second paragraph of the letter and the one that includes the reasons that attracted the candidate to the job position. This could be the perfect moment to briefly include the applicant's knowledge of the company.

Main Body

This is the **most important paragraph of the letter and the one that will guarantee the participation of the applicant in a possible job interview, if written correctly.** In this paragraph, the applicant should "sell" himself or herself using a positive and optimistic, but firm, language.

In the main body knowledge, abilities, achievements and challenges should be briefly included, **focusing them on the requirements of the company**. The candidate should **describe the attitudes and strengths of the applicants and how they could benefit the company further.**

Farewell

The farewell should be formal but friendly, avoiding typical sentences like "looking forward to hearing from you" but trying to be creative. A good idea is to include a sentence of the type **I will be willing to participate in any recruitment process or meeting that you should consider necessary**.

In the farewell, it is important to mention the dates when the applicant is **not** available for an interview with the idea of avoiding future problems of agenda.

Also, the applicant should thank the person for investing his or her time in the reading their letter and CV and, finally, sign the document.

CHAPTER VI: THE RESUME

On many occasions, companies and employment agencies ask the candidates to send a resume instead of a CV.

The resume is a document that is very similar to a CV with the difference that the first should not be longer than 1 single A4 page. In fact, the resume is a short curriculum and it is usually required by employment agencies and companies that receive a great number of applications and offer job positions regularly.

The information to include in the resume is the following:

- Personal details.

- Achievements, knowledge and skills.

- Academic details.

- Professional experience, including skills, strengths and achievements.

- Additional knowledge.

- Interests and hobbies (when related to the job position).

- References.

As the resume is a brief document, it is essential to have a good writing structure that provides fluidity to the reading and, as with a CV, the resume should be focused on each individual job position that the candidate applies for.

Some advice on elaborating the perfect resume includes:

1. Before you start writing the resume, develop the basic structure of the document. Therefore, a structure that includes a list of achievements, knowledge, skills, abilities, experience and challenges should be created.

2. It is important to build clear and concise sentences and use a formal, but friendly, vocabulary.

3. Also, it is essential to use action verbs like to develop, to build, to organise, to supervise or to manage.

4. The font of letter should be one that reads clearly enough and of a size between 10 and 14 (ideally size 12).

5. Never write a resume by hand, unless it is specifically required by the employer.

6. As with the CV, there are three types of resume: chronological (the most usual), functional (the most practical when the candidate does not have enough professional experience) and combined (the most complete).

7. Be optimistic and eliminate any information that could be negative. For example, data like age or reasons to leave previous job positions could sometimes play against the applicant.

8. It is fundamental to emphasise the strong points of the candidate (knowledge, abilities and achievements) focusing them to the job offered.

Finally, a last revision of the document is crucial in order to detect grammar and spelling mistakes. It is also important to check if all the necessary information has been introduced and whether or not any irrelevant information has been included.

It is a good idea to leave the document alone for two or three days before revising it again, and then it could be easier to detect possible mistakes.

9. Ask other people to read the document before sending it because, usually, a person that has nothing to do with the editing of the document could detect possible mistakes easily.

CHAPTER VII: THE APPLICATION FORM

Sometimes, companies prefer to use their own application forms instead of basing their decisions on CVs.

The reasons to favour application forms over CVs are various. With application forms, a company asks the candidate to give focused answers that the company believes are necessary. Therefore, the person in charge of granting the interview makes sure that he or she obtains the necessary information while not giving any chance to the applicant to include information that could be irrelevant.

There are a number of factors to consider at the time of filling in an application form:

1. Before filling the application form, you should obtain all the necessary information about the company and the offered job position.

2. The vocabulary to use should be direct and clear and, at the same time, informative.

3. The application form should be perfectly written without grammar or spelling mistakes.

4. Also, it is important to avoid studs or smudges.

   In many cases, the forms are available online and, therefore, it is recommended to print two or three copies that could be used as draft versions.

5. It is important that the application forms be filled in on a computer as it is easier to correct mistakes and it is possible to include longer texts in the different answers. However, it is fine (unlike with CVs, resume and presentation letters) to hand write an application form.

6. When more space is needed for the answers, it is possible to include additional sheets to further develop the list of knowledge, skills, achievements and experience.

7. It is necessary to avoid irrelevant information that is not related to the job position offered or that could result negatively during the recruitment process.

8. Also, it is fundamental to avoid including personal information such as religious or political beliefs.

9. Never write in a very narrative manner and introduce the information focusing on the outlined requirements.

10. If the candidate has to include interests and/or hobbies, it is important to mention those interests related to the job offered or that could provide positive information, avoiding the elaboration of a list such as "music, cinema, sport and reading". Instead, the applicant should try being a little more specific.

11. In the application forms it is necessary to include references. The ideal is that the references are provided by previous managers or supervisors. If the applicant has finished his or her studies recently, the references could be provided by either tutors or teachers.

12. In the application forms, there is a section to include previous professional experience, offering specific examples on the abilities and achievements required by the company.

   This is, definitively, the most difficult section of the application form but this is also the section that gives the candidate the chance of standing out among others.

Before writing this section, it is essential to develop a list of capabilities and achievements gained and challenges experienced during academic and professional life.

When the applicant does not have enough professional experience, it is a good idea to include volunteer work, internships and relevant courses.

The proper development of this section could, basically, guarantee a job interview for the candidate and, therefore, it is important to invest time and effort in the writing of this section.

In order to fill in this section successfully, the candidate should use the STAR method: Situation, Tasks, Action and Results.

Situation: The following questions should be answered: Where, When, How, With whom and For whom?

Tasks: Describe the situation in which the candidate found themselves in and the task to be developed.

Action: Describe, in a clear and concise manner, the decisions made and taken into practice.

Results: Describe the result and achievement obtained from including positive examples of successful results for the company.

For example, if the person has experience managing teams, and the application form requires giving examples of abilities to encourage the staff, the question could be developed as follows:

Situation: While working as Head of Department at... I had a team of 50 people working directly under my supervision.

Task: I was required to encourage the personnel.

Action: In this way, after analysing capabilities and strengths of each of the members of the staff, I decided to redistribute duties within the department depending on skills and preferences.

At the same time, I organised numerous meetings giving the staff the chance to offer their ideas and feelings as part of the project and the company.

Results: As a result, the staff felt more involved in the project and were more satisfied with their jobs and duties within the department, thus increasing their productivity.

Regular meetings with the staff facilitated their participation in the decision making process, making them feel more valued and creating a good job atmosphere and team spirit.

13. Once the application form is complete, it is a good idea to read it through, assuring that all the information introduced is correct and fixing any possible grammar and spelling mistakes you find.

14. Finally, save a copy that could be used as a base in a job interview.

CHAPTER VIII: APPENDIX AND EXAMPLES

As previously specified, there are three basic models of CV: chronological, functional and combined. The use of one or another option depends on the needs of the candidate.

CHRONOLOGICAL CURRICULUM 1

Name and Surname

Address - Telephone and email

Professional Objectives: Brief description of knowledge, achievements and challenges.

Professional Experience (from present to past)

Date and **Name of the company**

Job position

- Description of duties
- Description of duties

Date and **Name of the company**

Job position

- Description of duties
- Description of duties

Academic Formation

Date and **Name of the academic institution**

Qualification and final marks.

Date and **Name of the academic institution**

Qualification and final marks.

Additional Academic Information (additional courses)

Date and **Title of the course**, seminar or conference

Duration of the course

Additional Knowledge

Computing Skills: Programme and level

Interests and Hobbies

Include interests and hobbies when related to the position.

CHRONOLOGICAL CURRICULUM 2

Name and Surname

Address - Telephone and email

Professional Objectives: Brief description of knowledge, achievements and professional challenges.

Professional Experience (from present to past)

Date and **Name of the company**

Job position

- Description of duties
- Description of duties

Date and **Name of the company**

Job position

- Description of duties

Academic Formation

Date and **Name of the academic institution**

Qualification and final marks

Date and **Name of the academic institution**

Qualification and final marks

Additional Academic Information (additional courses)

Date and **Title of the course**, seminar or conference

Duration of the course

Date and **Title of the course**, seminar or conference

Duration of the course

Computing Skills	**Languages**	**Other information**
Programme and level	Language and level	Driving license Time flexibility

EXAMPLE OF CHRONOLOGICAL CV

Marilyn Harris

98 Gaynor Street, SW1V London

Telephone: 0207 XXXXXX Email: xxxx@gmail.com

Professional Objectives: Executive with five years of experience in the administration area and an ability to work under pressure. My goal is to provide my experience and knowledge to your company.

Professional Experience (from present to past)

2011- 2003 **Sycernatic Ltd.**

Personal Assistant

Duties:

- Organisation of meetings and events
- Elaboration and translation of documents

2003-2001   **Mars Consultancy**

Administrator

Duties:

- Supervision and updating of extensive database
- Taking care of the accountancy of the department

Education

2001-1996 **University of London**

BA in Business Administration. Final Mark: 2.1

Additional Academic Information

2002 **Course in Marketing Expert**

- Marketing techniques and organization of events
- Elaboration of business plans

Computing Skills: Microsoft Office, expert level

EXAMPLE OF FUNCTIONAL CURRICULUM

Name and Surname

Address- Telephone and email

Professional Objectives

Brief description of knowledge, achievements and professional challenges

Abilities and Achievements

Capability 1

Abilities: Briefing of professional capabilities

Achievements: Achievements focused on this skill

Capability 2

Abilities: Briefing of professional capabilities

Achievements: Achievements focused on this skill

Education

2001-1996 **Name of the academic institution**

Qualification and final mark

1996-1995 **Name of the academic institution**

Qualification and final mark

Professional Internship

Date and **Name of the company**

Title of the job position

- Description of duties

Date and **Name of the company**

Title of the job position

- Description of duties
- Description of duties

Computing Skills: Programme and level

EXAMPLE OF FUNCTIONAL CURRICULUM
Name and Surname

Address
Telephone and email

Abilities and Achievements

Capability 1
Abilities: Briefing of professional capabilities
Achievements: Achievements focused on this skill

Capability 2
Abilities: Briefing of professional capabilities
Achievements: Achievements focused on this skill

Capability 3
Abilities: Briefing of professional capabilities
Achievements: Achievements focused on this skill

Professional Experience

Date and **Name of the company**

Title of the job position

- Description of duties
- Description of duties

Academic Education

Date and **Name of the academic institution**

Qualification and final mark

Date and **Name of the academic institution**

Qualification and final mark

Computing Skills	**Languages**	**Other information**
Programme and level	Language and level	Driving license

EXAMPLE OF FUNCTIONAL CURRICULUM

Marilyn Harris

98 Gaynor Street, SW1V London Phone: 0207 xxxxxx

Professional Objectives

After finishing a BSc in Finances, I wish to formulate a career in business. I consider myself a responsible professional with great ability to coordinate teams.

Abilities and Achievements

Communication capability

Great negotiation skills and the ability to deal with people, organising international events and taking care of the external communications.

Team work

Working as a part of a team has allowed me to obtain a large number of professional objectives and achievements.

Professional Internship

2003-2001 Mars Consultancy

Event Assistant

- Customer assistant and information
- Organisation of events and resolution of problems

Academic Education

2001-1996 University of London

BSc in Business Administration

Average mark: B

Additional Academic Information

2002 Course of Marketing Expert

200 hours

- Marketing techniques and events organisation
- Development of business plans

EXAMPLE OF COMBINED CURRICULUM 1

Name and Surname

Address - Telephone and email

Professional Objectives

Description of knowledge, achievements and challenges

Abilities and Achievements

Capability 1

Abilities: Briefing of professional capabilities

Achievements: Achievements focused on this skill

Capability 2

Abilities: Briefing of professional capabilities

Achievements: Achievements focused on this skill

Capability 3

Abilities: Briefing of professional capabilities

Achievements: Achievements focused on this skill

Education

2001-1996 **Name of the academic institution**

Qualification and final mark

1996-1995 **Name of the academic institution**

Qualification and final mark

Professional Experience (from present to past)

Date and **Name of the company**

Job position

- Description of duties
- Description of duties

Date and **Name of the company**

Job position

- Description of duties
- Description of duties

Computing Skills: Programme and level

Languages: Language and level

EXAMPLE OF COMBINED CURRICULUM 2

Photo **Name and Surname** Address Telephone Mobile E-mail	**Professional Objectives** Description of knowledge, achievements and professional goals **Abilities and Achievements** **Capability 1** Abilities: Briefing of professional capabilities Achievements: Briefing of achievements focused on this skill **Capability 2** Abilities: Briefing of professional capabilities Achievements: Achievements focused on this skill **Capability 3** Abilities: Briefing of professional capabilities Achievements: Achievements focused on this skill

Professional Experience (present to past)

Date   **Name of the company**
        Job position
        - Description of duties
        - Description of duties

Date   **Name of the company**
        Job position
        - Description of duties
        - Description of duties

Academic Formation

Dates   **Name of the institution**
        Qualification and final marks.

Date   **Name of the institution**
        Qualification and final marks.

Computing Skills: Programme and level
                     Programme and level

Languages: Language and level

References: Available on request

EXAMPLE OF COMBINED CURRICULUM

Marilyn Harris

98 Gaynor Street, SW1V London - Phone.: 0207 xxxxxx

Professional Objectives

After finishing a BSc in Economics, I wish to develop a career in the business sector. I consider myself a responsible professional with the great ability to make decisions while coordinating other teams and departments.

Abilities and Achievements

Communication capability

Great negotiation skills and an ability to deal with people, organising international events.

Analysis and strategic thinking

Resolution of complex problems through different analysis.

Professional Experience (from present to past)

2011-2003 **Sycernatic Ltd.**

Personal Assistant

Duties:

- Organisations of meetings and events
- Editing and translation of documents

2003-2001 **Mars Consultancy**

Administrator

Duties:

- Supervision and updating of extensive database
- Organisation of events and resolution of problems

Education

2001-1996 **University of London**

BSc in Business Administration

Average mark: B

Languages: English, advanced level

EXAMPLE OF RESUME

Name and Surname

Address _ Telephone and email

Professional Objectives: Brief description of knowledge, achievements and professional challenges.

Professional Experience (from present to past)

Date and **Name of the company**

Job position

- Description of duties

Date and **Name of the company**

Job position

- Description of duties
- Description of duties

Education

Date and **Name of the academic institution**

Qualification and final marks

Computing Skills: Programme and level

EXAMPLE OF RESUME
Name and Surname
Address, telephone and email

Skills and Achievements
Capability 1
Abilities: Briefing of professional capabilities
Achievements: Achievements focused on this skill
Capability 2
Abilities: Briefing of professional capabilities
Achievements: Achievements focused on this skill

Education
Date and **Name of the institution**
Qualification and final mark

Internship
Date and **Name of the company**
Job position
- Description of duties

EXAMPLE OF RESUME

Marilyn Harris

98 Gaynor Street, SW1V- London Telephone: 0207 xxxxxx

Communication skills: Dealing with customers in international congresses while developing profound communication skills.

Organisation and leadership skills: Participation in the development and coordination of congresses and conferences.

Professional Experience (from present to past)

2011-2003 **Sycernatic Ltd.**

Personal Assistant

- Organisation of meetings and events
- Editing and translation of documents

2003-2001 **Mars Consulting**

Administrator

- Development of extensive databases
- Communication with clients and suppliers

Academic Education

2001-1996 **University of London**

BSc in Business Administration

Final mark: B

EXAMPLE OF COVER LETTER

Name and Surname
Address
Telephone and email

Name, surname and job position of the person in charge of the recruitment process or the name of the company.

First paragraph: Specify the desired job position and how the candidate found out about it.

Second paragraph: Specify the reasons why the candidate is interested in the job position and mention that the CV is included.

Third paragraph: Briefing of abilities and achievements focused on the job position offered.

Fourth paragraph: Thank the person for his or her time and specify when the candidate will not be available for an interview or meeting.

Goodbye paragraph: Formal and polite. Sign the document.

EXAMPLE OF COVER LETTER

Marilyn Harris
98 Gaynor Street, SW1V- London

John J. Smith- Head of Human Resources

Dear Mr. Smith,

I write to you regarding the position of Academic Manager, published last Monday in the newspaper XXX. As you could see from my attached CV, I have extensive experience coordinating academic departments and this is the main reason why I felt attracted to this job position.

I have experience, as required, for academic projects and personnel, developing all types of documents, conferences and study programmes while distributing duties among the staff under my supervision.

I will participate in any meeting or recruitment process that you consider necessary. Thank you for your time and consideration.

Yours sincerely,
Marilyn Harris

SPONTANEOUS COVER LETTER

Marilyn Harris
98 Gaynor Street, SW1V- London
Telephone: 0207 xxxxxx Email:xxxx@gmail.com

John J. Smith- Head of Human Resources

Dear Mr. Smith,

I have learnt about the activity developed by your organisation thanks to my previous professional experience. As you could see from my attached CV, I have a BA in English Language and experience of taking on board research projects. I have elaborated articles and edited all kinds of documents while searching for new funding sources and organising conferences.

I will participate in any meeting or recruitment process that you consider necessary. Please, do not hesitate to contact me if additional information is required. Thank you for your time and consideration.

Yours sincerely,
Marilyn Harris

Printed in Poland
by Amazon Fulfillment
Poland Sp. z o.o., Wrocław